The ONE TRUE GOD

and the plagues of Egypt...

A song written and performed
by Ahava L / Notable Praise

Hebrew Helps:

Avraham   /Av-ra-ham/ (Abraham)

Elohim   /Eh – lo – heem/
    (Title of the Creator in Genesis 1:1)

Mitzraim   /Meetz – rah – yeem/ (Egypt)

moed   /mo-ed/   (Appointed Time)

Nissan   /Ni-san/
    (first month of Biblical year –
    also referred to as "Aviv")

Yaakov   /Ya-a-kov/ (Jacob)

Yitzkhak   /Yeetz- khak/   (Isaac)

Yisrael   /Yees- ra-el/ (Israel)

ISBN 978-1-945563-38-6

Minister2Others.com

Passover is the time to remember
That we are slaves no more!
The matza, the bitter herbs,
The blood upon our doors...

What יהוה did in Egypt

We speak of this moed
He is the only One True God
And there none but Him!

On the fourteenth day of Nissan
יהוה passed over me

He took the firstborn Mitzrayim

And set the captives free

He came against all their false gods

And proved that only He

Is the One True God!

The God of Avraham

Is the One True God!

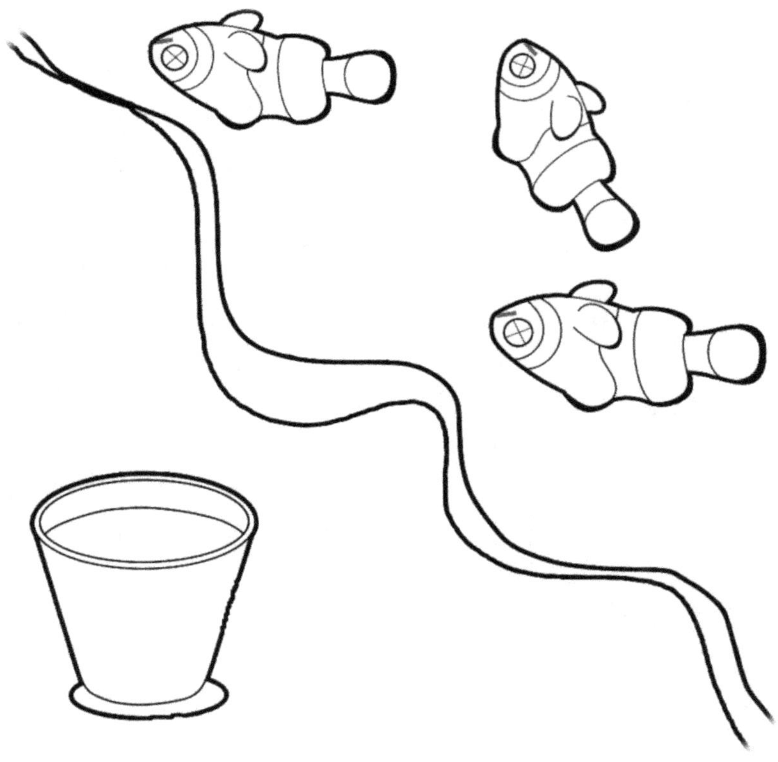

He turned the water into blood

And made all their fish die

He sent the frogs upon the shores

And turned the dust to lice

The magicians tried to do the same

But they could not so they cried,

"This is the finger of God!"

The God of Yitzkhak

Is the One True God!

God made a distinction

Our Father drew a line

He said,

"Swarms come on your people,

But they won't come on Mine!"

After that a sickness came

And all their cattle died

Our God is the One True God!

The God of Yaakov

Is the One True God!

Ashes from the furnace

Became boils in the land

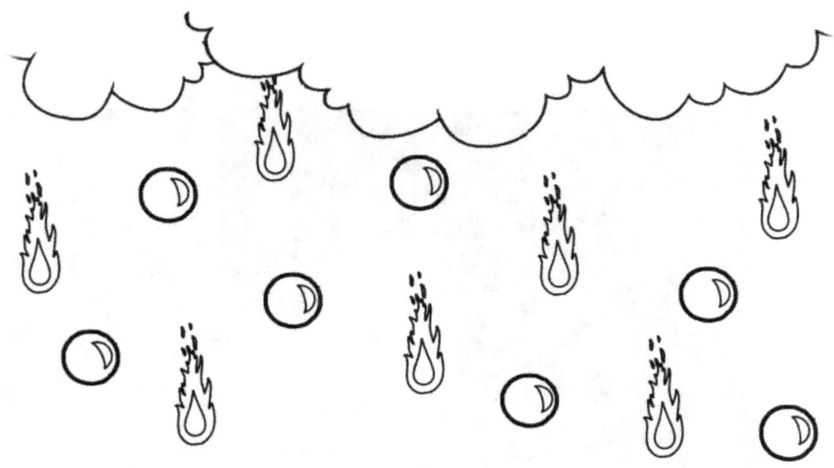

Hail and fire poured as rain

And locust ate the flax

Darkness came then death to those

Who brushed off the command

Of the One True God

The God of Yisrael

Is the One True God!

שְׁמַ֖ע
יִשְׂרָאֵ֑ל
יְהֹוָה
אֱלֹהֵ֖ינוּ
יְהֹוָה
אֶחָֽד

Hear, O Yisrael,
יהוה is our God!

יהוה alone!